_____

(a word to describe me)

_____

(my name)

My progress chart

Find the letter to match your completed page. Track the letter and colour the picture.

Help each animal find its way.

Track.

Trace.

Copy.

Track.

Trace.

Copy.

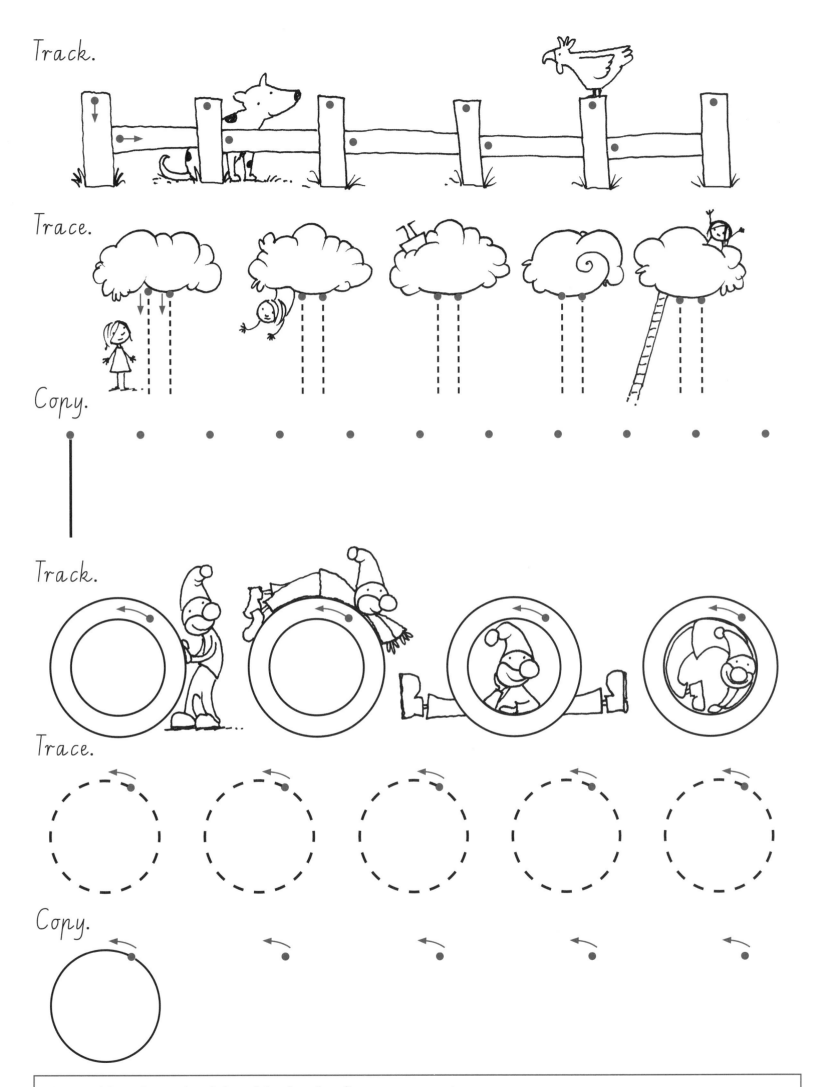

Trace.

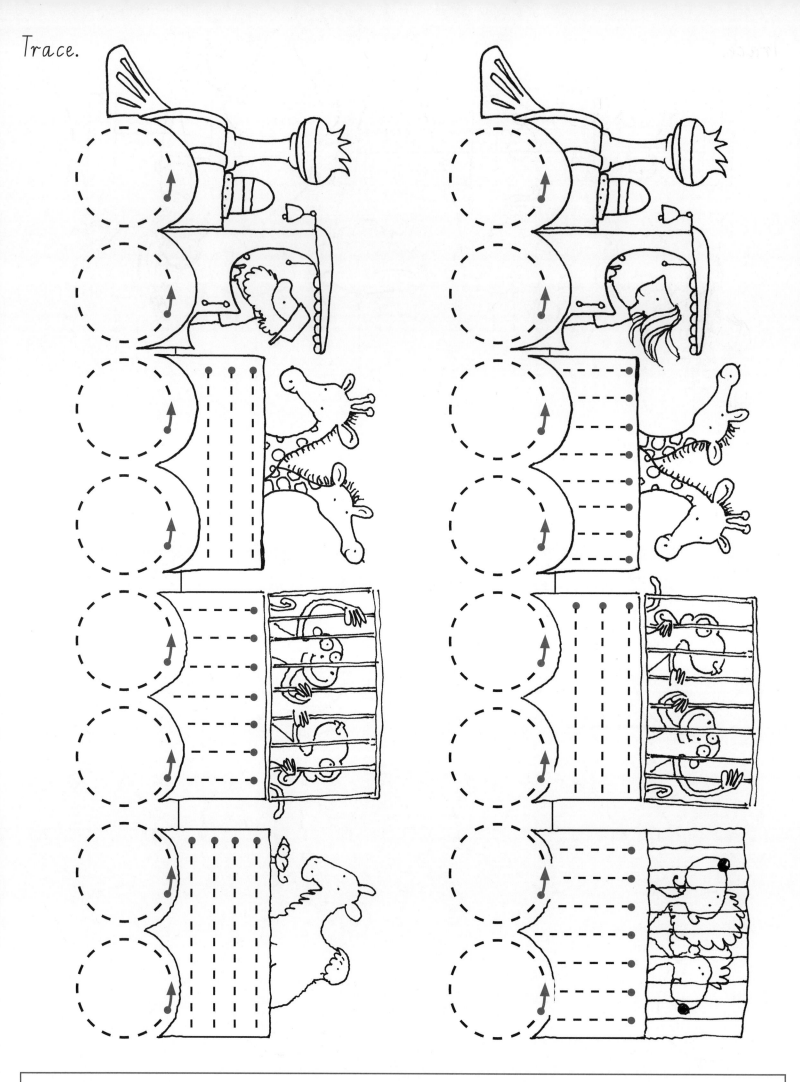

Handwriting: Patterning, downstroke and anticlockwise movements, left to right direction, fine motor control.

6

Trace.

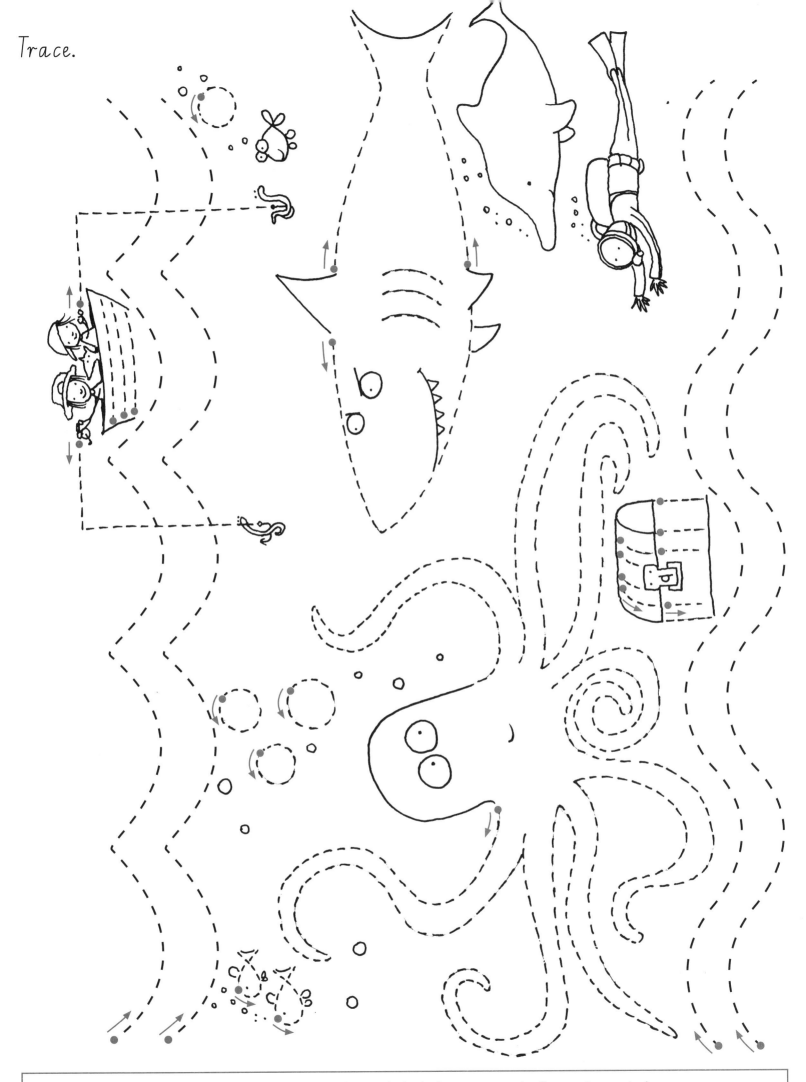

Handwriting: Patterning, downstroke, anticlockwise and clockwise movements, fine motor control.

7

Track the pattern. Keep your pencil on the page.

Trace the pattern. Keep your pencil on the page.

Trace the pattern.

Track.

Handwriting: anticlockwise letter, body letter (a).
Vocabulary on page: ant, anteater, angry, alligator.
Extra vocabulary: an, are, apple, cat, mat, sat, tap.

Track.

Trace.

Trace.

Write.

Patter Start at one o'clock. Go left then curve down, around the bottom and back up to the start, then straight down and go up to exit. Keep your pencil on the page.

Chant:

cool cow

c c c

Trace the pattern.

Find c.

Track.

Handwriting: anticlockwise letter, body letter (c).
Vocabulary on page: cool, cow, cat, cup, cake, candle.
Extra vocabulary: cold.

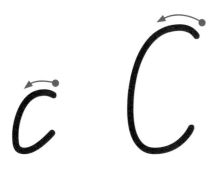 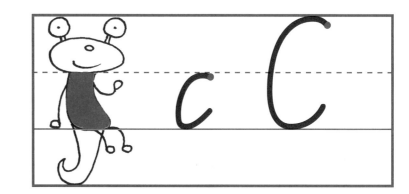

Track.

Trace.

Trace.

 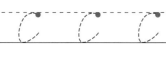 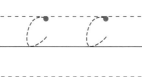 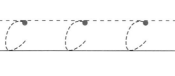 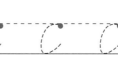 

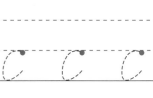

Write.

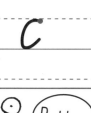 Patter Start at one o'clock. Go left then curve down, around the bottom and up about halfway. Keep your pencil on the page.

dirty dog
d d d

Trace the pattern.

Trace the pattern.

Track.

Handwriting: anticlockwise letter, head and body letter (d).
Vocabulary on page: dog, dirty.
Extra vocabulary: do, don't, done, dip, lid, pad, down.

12

d D

Track.

d d d d d d

Trace.

d d d d d d

Trace.

d d d d d d d d d d d

d d d d d d d d d d d

Write.

d

d

Patter Start at one o'clock. Go left then curve down, around the bottom and up all the way to the top, then straight down and go up to exit. Keep your pencil on the page.

Chant:

giggly goanna

g g g

Trace the pattern.

Trace the pattern.

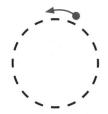  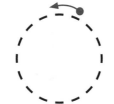 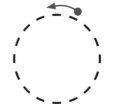  

Trace the pattern.

Track.

    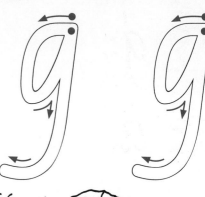

Handwriting: anticlockwise letter, body and tail letter (g).
Vocabulary on page: giggly, goanna.
Extra vocabulary: get, go, got, pig, dig, dog, hog, jog, egg.

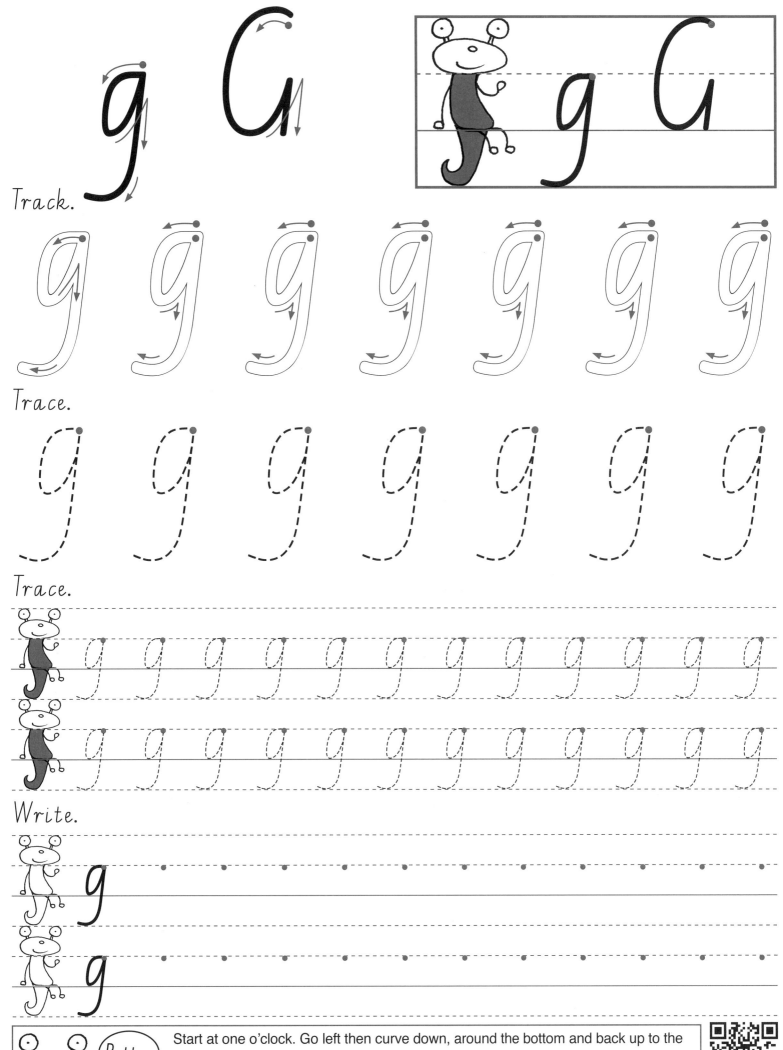

Track.

Trace.

Trace.

Write.

 Start at one o'clock. Go left then curve down, around the bottom and back up to the start, then straight down and go left to make a tail. Keep your pencil on the page.

Trace the pattern. Keep your pencil on the page.

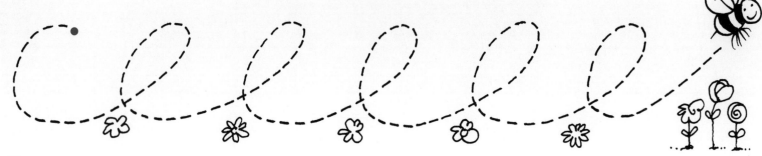

Trace the pattern. Keep your pencil on the page.

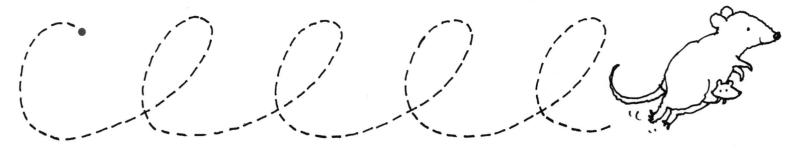

Trace.

Track.

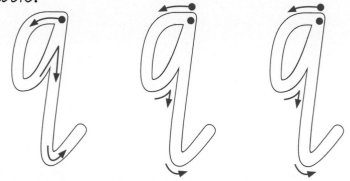

Handwriting: anticlockwise letter, body and tail letter (q).
Vocabulary on page: quick, quokkas.
Extra vocabulary: quack, queen.

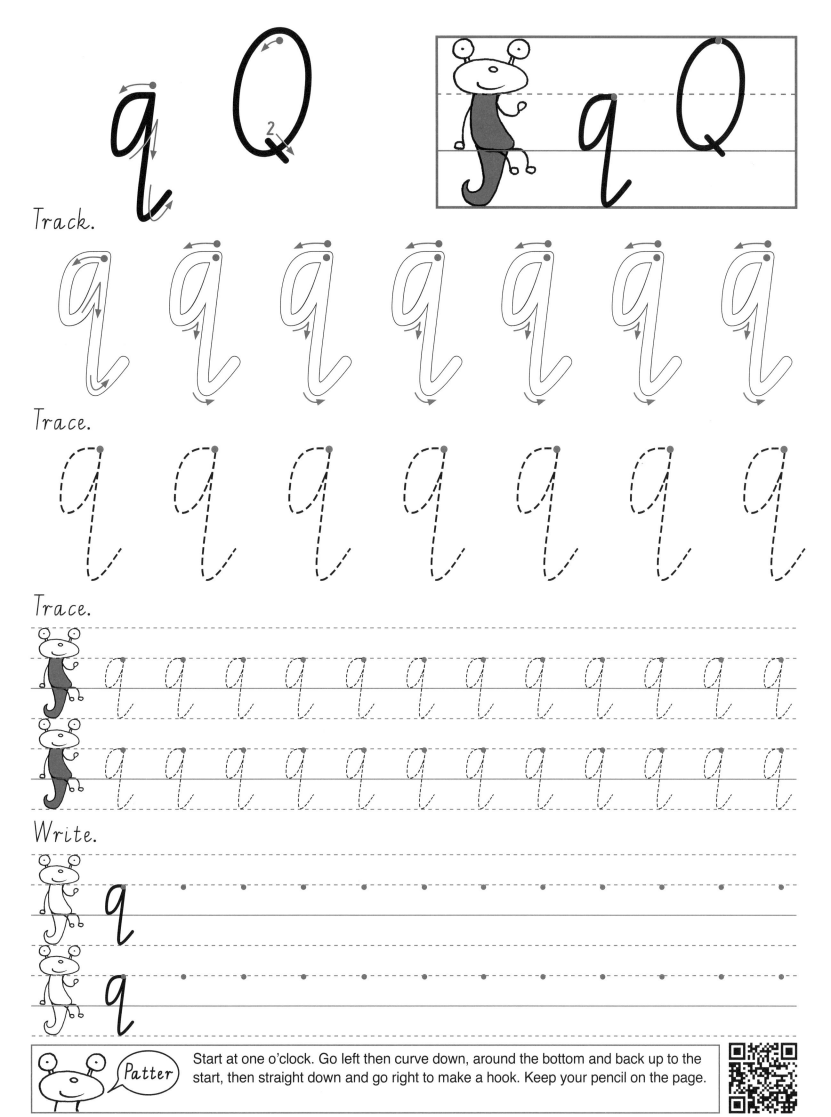

Track.

Trace.

Trace.

Write.

Patter — Start at one o'clock. Go left then curve down, around the bottom and back up to the start, then straight down and go right to make a hook. Keep your pencil on the page.

Trace the pattern. Keep your pencil on the page.

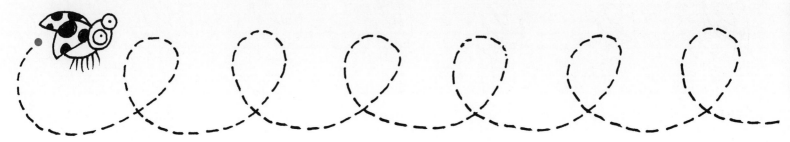

Trace the pattern.

Trace the pattern.

Track.

Handwriting: anticlockwise letter, body letter (e).
Vocabulary on page: egg, eagle, beetle, elephant, energetic.
Extra vocabulary: eat, he, she, the, red, net, yell, men.

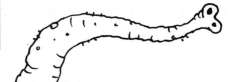

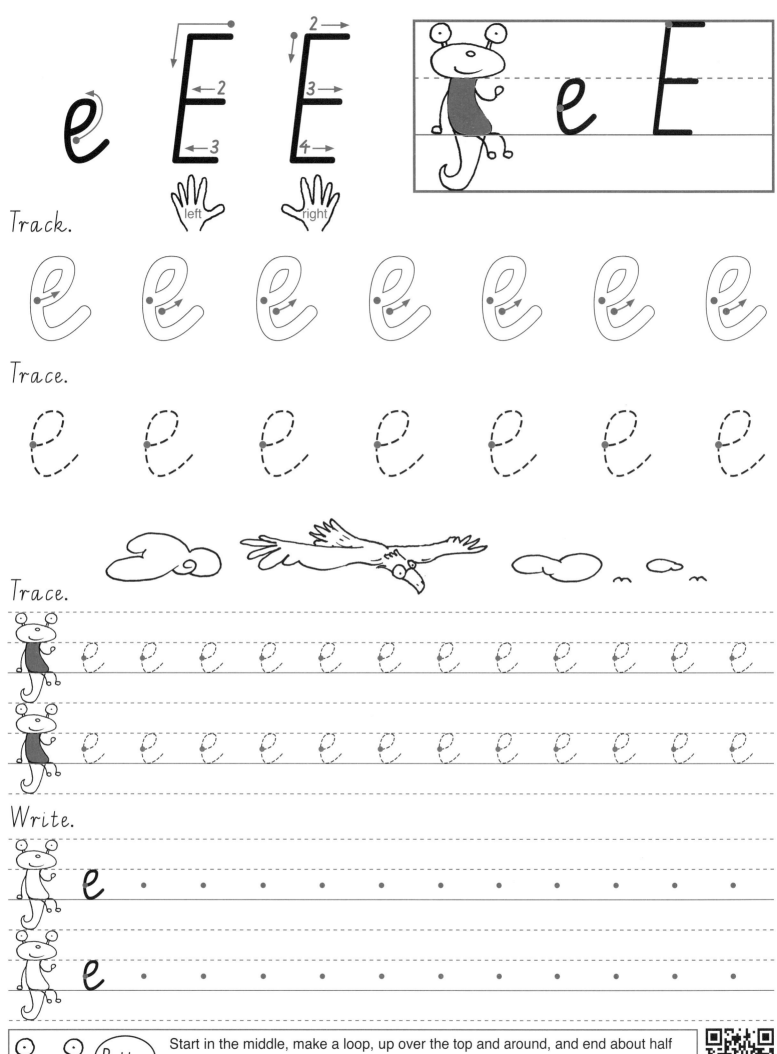

Track.

Trace.

Trace.

Write.

Start in the middle, make a loop, up over the top and around, and end about half way up the space. Keep your pencil on the page.

Patter

19

Chant:

orange octopus
o o o

Trace the pattern.

Trace the pattern. Keep your pencil on the page.

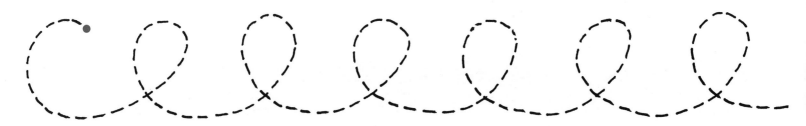

Trace the pattern.

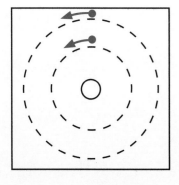 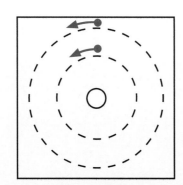 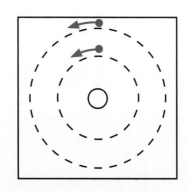 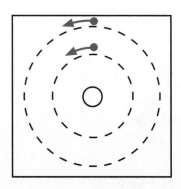

Track.

Handwriting: anticlockwise letter, body letter (o).
Vocabulary on page: orange, octopus.
Extra vocabulary: on, not, hot, pot, of, to, log, pop, stop, go, no.

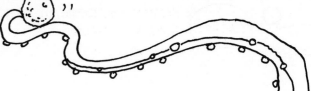

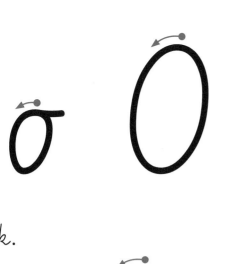
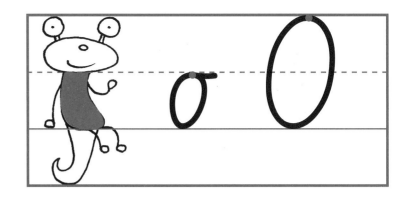

Track.

Trace.

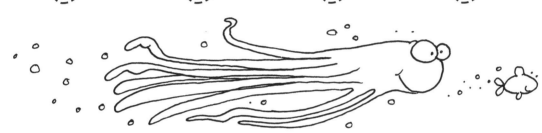

Trace.

 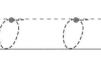 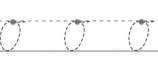 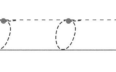 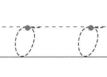 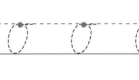

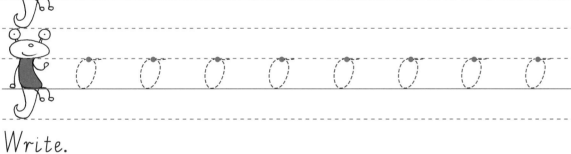

Write.

 O

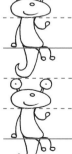 O

 (Patter) Start at 12 o'clock. Go left then curve down, around the bottom and up to join where you started and go right to exit. Keep your pencil on the page.

Chant:

frisky frog
f f f

Trace the pattern.

Trace the pattern. Keep your pencil on the page.

Find and write f.

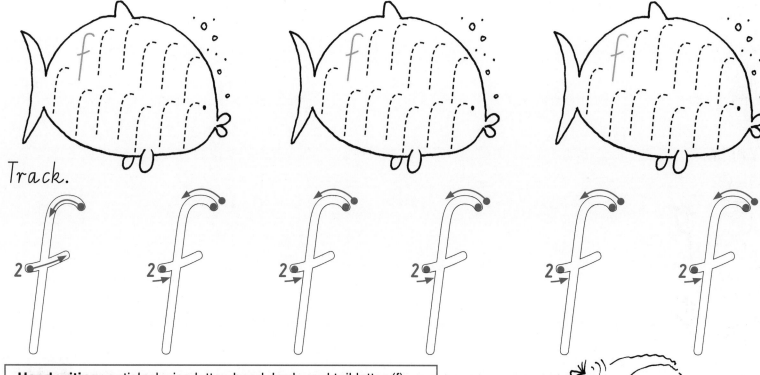

Track.

Handwriting: anticlockwise letter, head, body and tail letter (f).
Vocabulary on page: frog, fish, flower, frisky.
Extra vocabulary: fun, fin, fan.

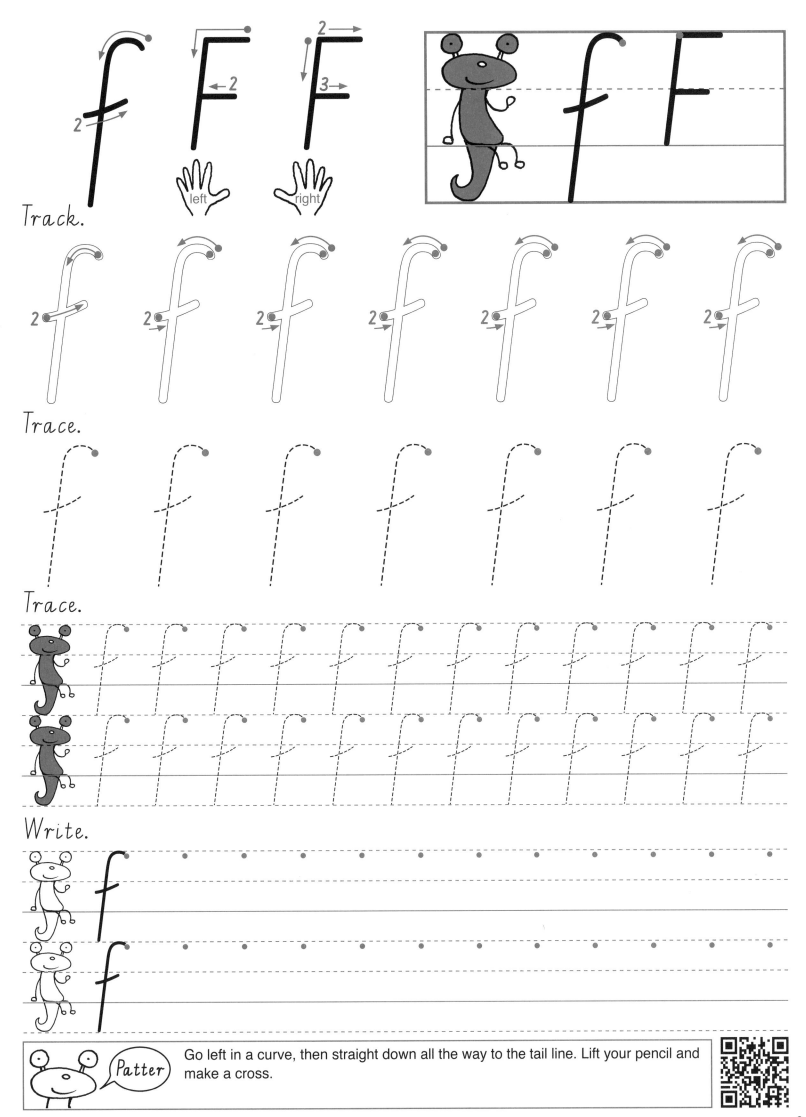

Track.

Trace.

Trace.

Write.

Patter Go left in a curve, then straight down all the way to the tail line. Lift your pencil and make a cross.

Trace the pattern.

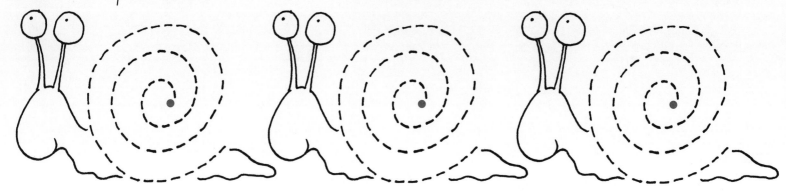

Trace the pattern. Turn the pattern into snakes.

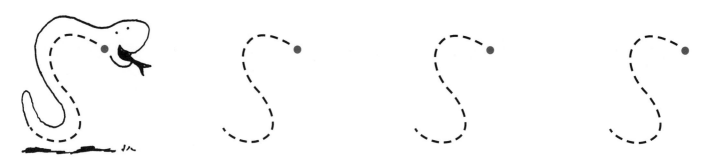

Trace the pattern. Keep your pencil on the page.

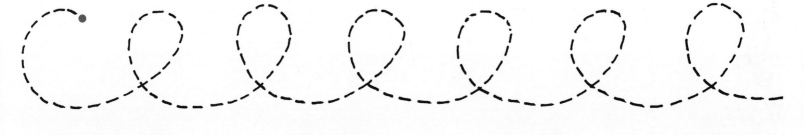

Track.

Handwriting: anticlockwise letter, body letter (s).
Vocabulary on page: snake, snail, seal, shear, slippery, scissors.
Extra vocabulary: so, sit, sat, yes, six, sun, shut, shop, slip.

Track.

Trace.

Trace.

Write.

First go left, then curve around and across the middle, then go around the bottom and go left to exit. Keep your pencil on the page.

25

Chant:

messy monkey
m m m

Trace the pattern.

 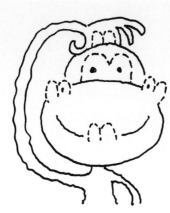  

Trace the pattern. Keep your pencil on the page.

m m m m

Trace the pattern. Turn each pattern into a picture.

Track.

Handwriting: clockwise letter with rounded entry, body letter (m).
Vocabulary on page: messy, monkey.
Extra vocabulary: mat, mop, man, am, mum, men, him, many, munch.

m M M 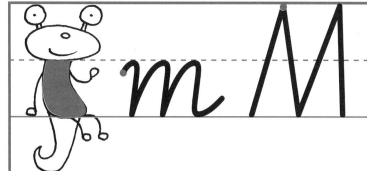 *m M*

Track.

m   m   m   m

Trace.

m   m   m   m

Trace.

m m m m m m m m m m

m m m m m m m

Write.

m

m

Enter up then go down, bounce up and across the top and make a second downstroke, then bounce up and across the top and make a third downstroke and go up to exit. Keep your pencil on the page.

27

Track the pattern.

Trace the pattern. Keep your pencil on the page.

Copy the pattern. Turn each pattern into a picture.

Track.

Handwriting: clockwise letter with rounded entry, body letter (n).
Vocabulary on page: noisy, numbat.
Extra vocabulary: no, not, nap, nip, nod, can, sun, run.

28

n N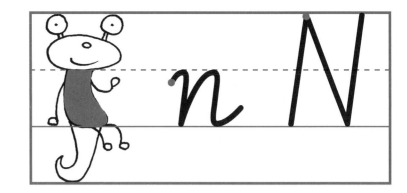

Track.

Trace.

Trace.

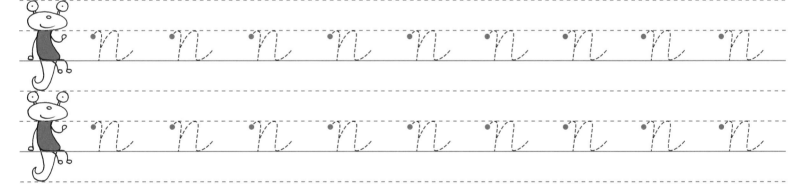

Write.

Patter Enter up then go down, then up and across the top and down again. Go up to exit. Keep your pencil on the page.

rapid rat
r r r

Trace the pattern.

Find r.

r ⌐⌐⌐⌐⌐⌐⌐⌐⌐⌐

Track.

Handwriting: clockwise letter with rounded entry, body letter (r).
Vocabulary on page: rat, race, rapid.
Extra vocabulary: rip, run, ran, raft.

 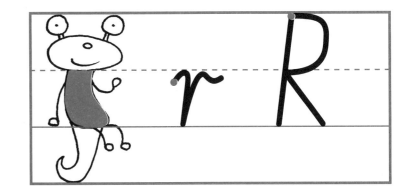

Track.

Trace.

Trace.

   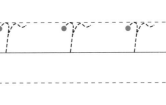 

Write.

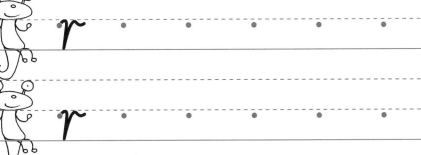

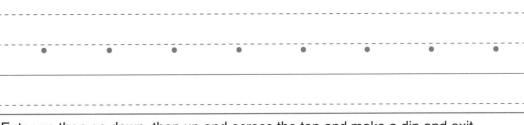

 Enter up then go down, then up and across the top and make a dip and exit.
Keep your pencil on the page.

foxy ox
x x x

Track the pattern.

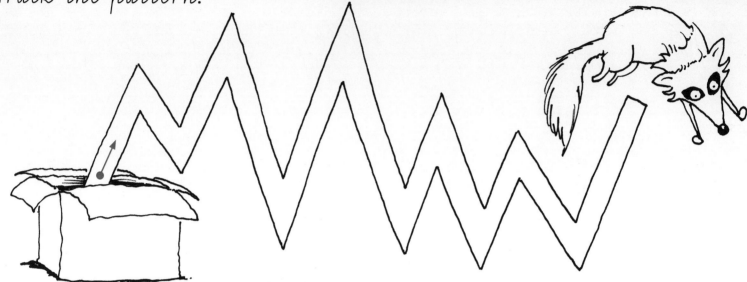

Trace the pattern. Keep your pencil on the page.

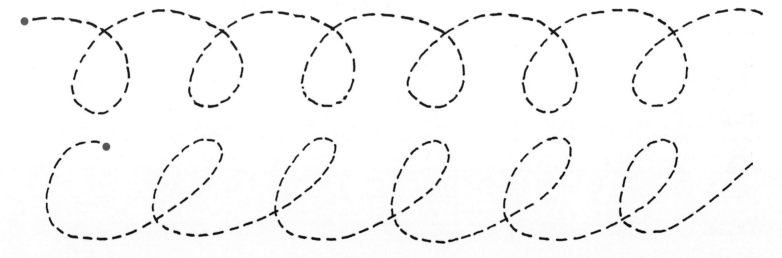

Track.

Handwriting: clockwise letter with rounded entry, body letter (x).
Vocabulary on page: ox, box, fox, foxy.
Extra vocabulary: x-ray.

32

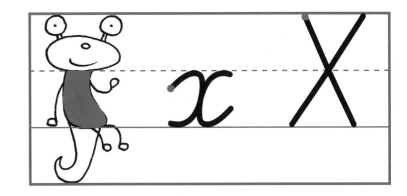

Track.

Trace.

Trace.

 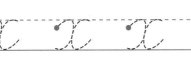 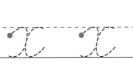 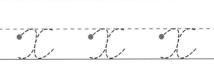

Write.

 Start at the top left, curve around and down, then go left to exit. Lift your pencil.
Go to the top right. Curve around and down and go right to exit.

33

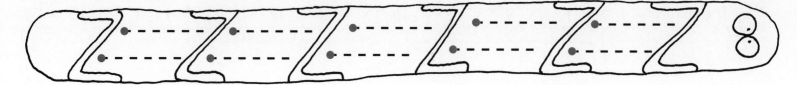

zigzag zebra
3 3 3

Trace the pattern.

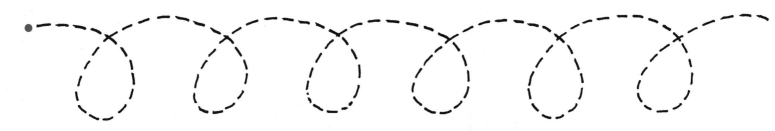

Trace the pattern.

Find z.

Track.

Handwriting: clockwise letter with rounded entry, body and tail letter (z).
Vocabulary on page: zebra, zigzag.
Extra vocabulary: zoo, zoom, zap, zip, zipper, jazz, pizza.

3 Z

Track.

Trace.

Trace.

Write.

Go up, around and down to the baseline. Then go up, around and down and go left to make a tail. Keep your pencil on the page.

hairy hen
h h h

Trace the pattern.

Trace the pattern. Keep your pencil on the page.

Trace then copy the pattern.

Track.

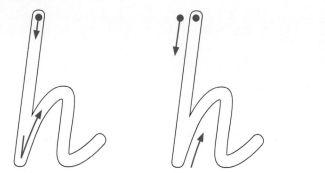

Handwriting: clockwise letter, head and body letter (h).
Vocabulary on page: hen, hay, hairy.
Extra vocabulary: hop, help, has, hat, hot, he, she, him, have.

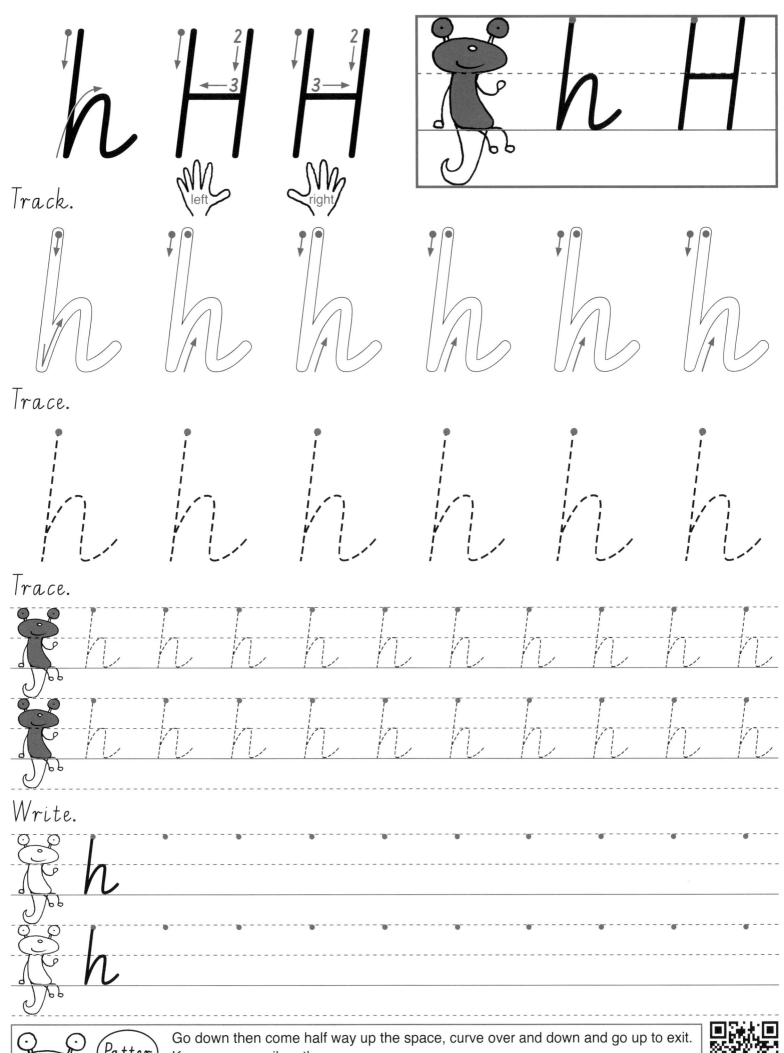

Track.

Trace.

Trace.

Write.

Patter Go down then come half way up the space, curve over and down and go up to exit.
Keep your pencil on the page.

37

Trace the pattern. Finish the kites.

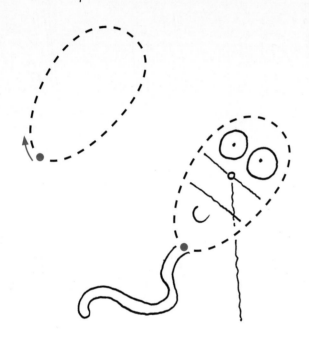

Trace the pattern.

Track.

Handwriting: clockwise letter, head and body letter (k).
Vocabulary on page: kind, koala, kite.
Extra vocabulary: kit, kitten, king, kangaroo, key.

k K²

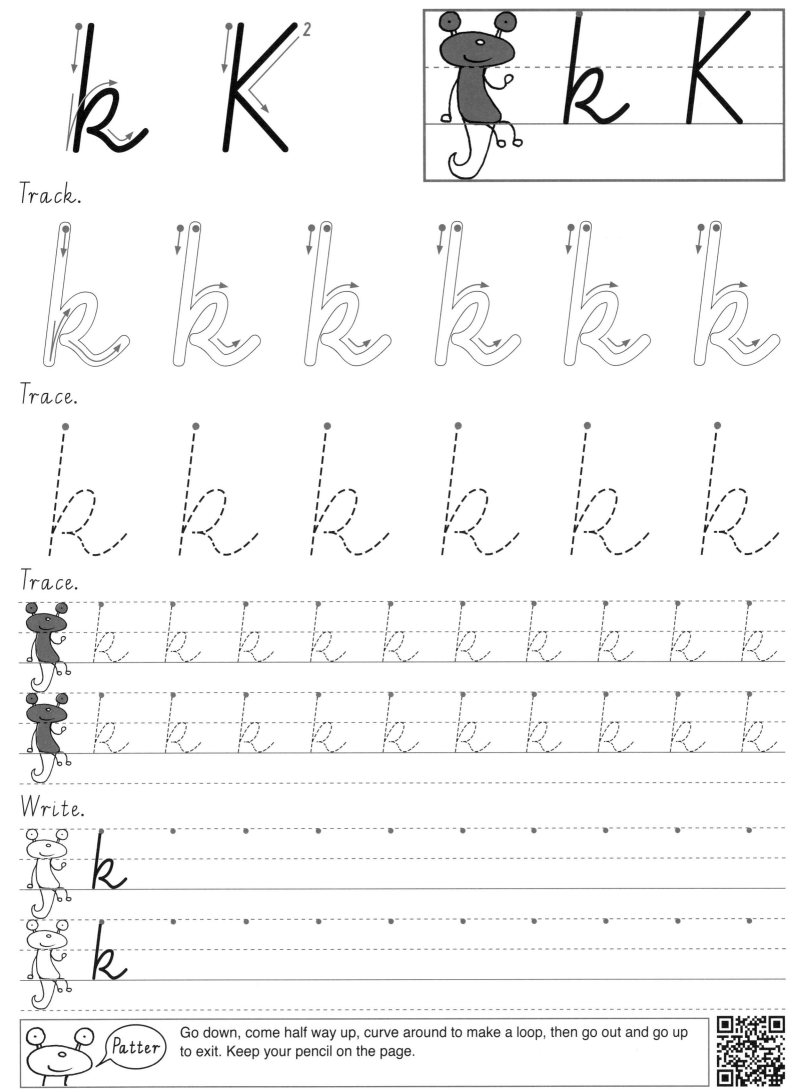

Track.

Trace.

Trace.

Write.

Patter — Go down, come half way up, curve around to make a loop, then go out and go up to exit. Keep your pencil on the page.

Chant:

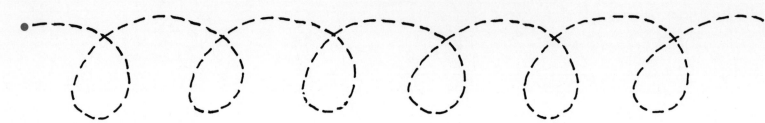

Trace the pattern. Keep your pencil on the page.

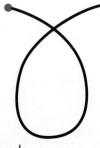

Trace the patterns.

Copy the pattern.

Track.

Handwriting: clockwise letter, body and tail letter (p).
Vocabulary on page: pig, pretty.
Extra vocabulary: pat, pot, put, pan, pop, map, nip, top, pink.

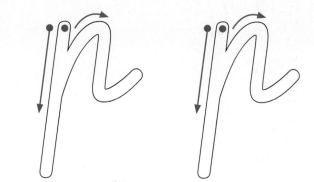

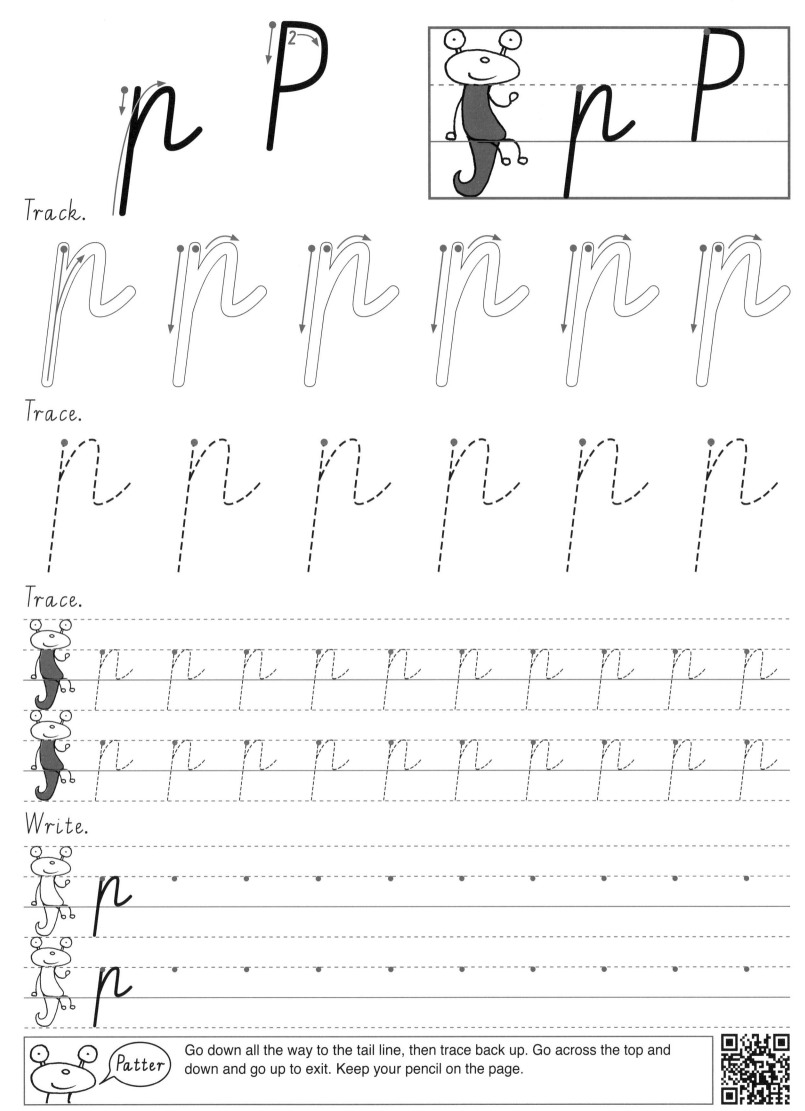

Track.

Trace.

Trace.

Write.

Patter — Go down all the way to the tail line, then trace back up. Go across the top and down and go up to exit. Keep your pencil on the page.

Chant:

itchy iguana

i i i

Trace the pattern.

Trace.

Trace.

Track.

2⊙　2⊙　2⊙　2⊙　2⊙　2⊙　2⊙

Handwriting: i family letter, body letter (i).
Vocabulary on page: insect, itchy, iguana.
Extra vocabulary: I, is, it, in, if, six, will, sit, lip.

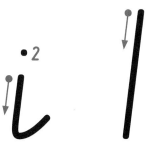 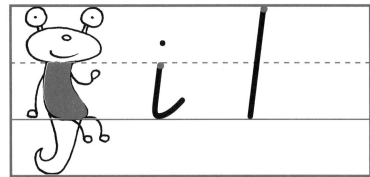

Trace the pattern. Keep your pencil on the page.

Copy the pattern.

illi

Trace.

Write.

Go straight down, then go up to exit. Lift your pencil and add a dot.

Patter

43

Trace the pattern.

Find and write t.

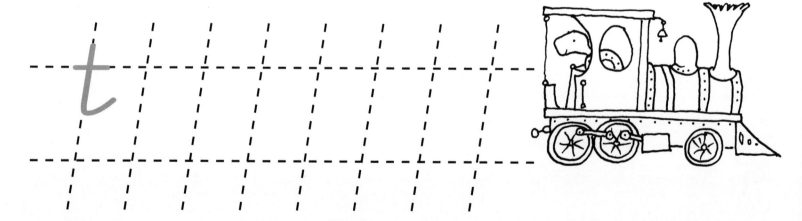

Track.

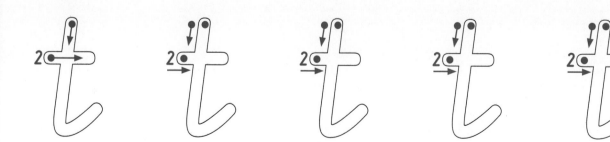

Handwriting: i family letter, head and body letter (t).
Vocabulary on page: track, train, tree, turtle, tidy, tortoise.
Extra vocabulary: tap, tip, ten, it, at, hot, get, pet, net.

44

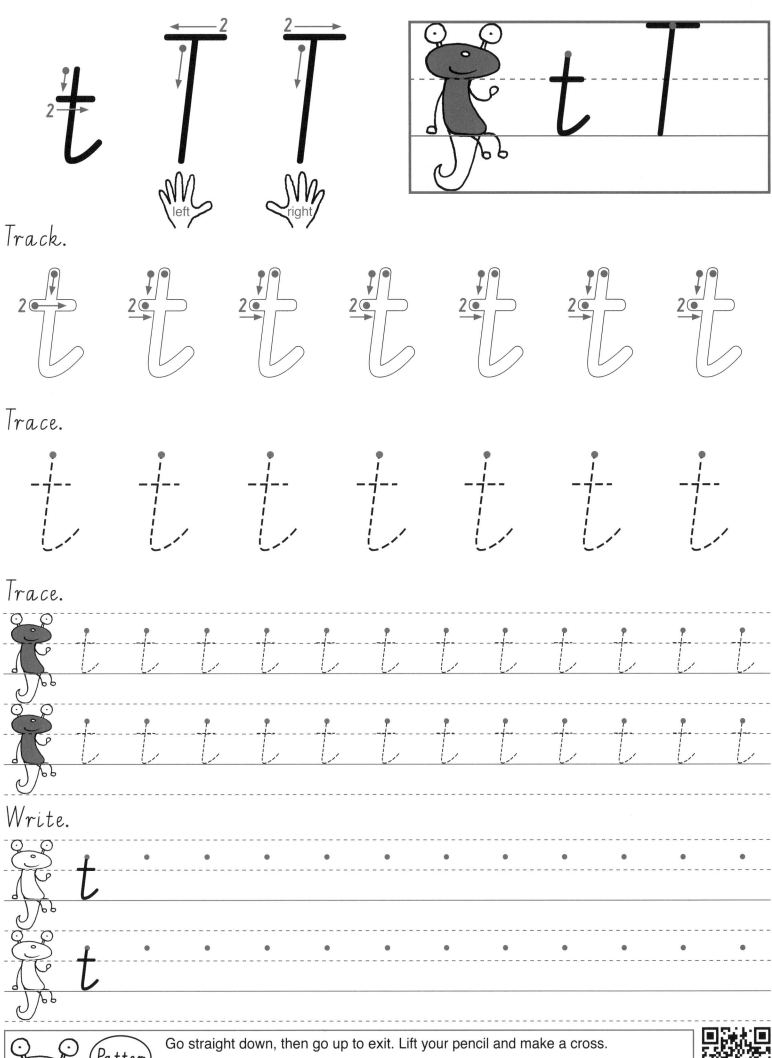

Track.

Trace.

Trace.

Write.

 Go straight down, then go up to exit. Lift your pencil and make a cross.

Trace the pattern.

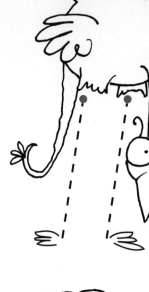

Trace the pattern.

Track.

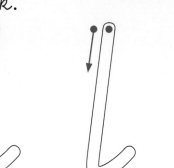
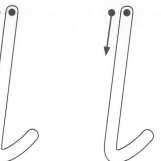
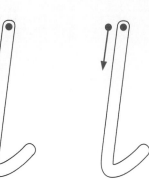
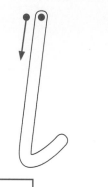
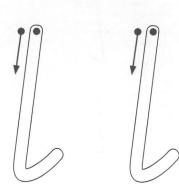

Handwriting: i family letter, head and body letter (l).
Vocabulary on page: leg, lion, lazy.
Extra vocabulary: lot, love, little, like, light.

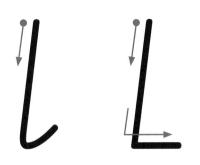

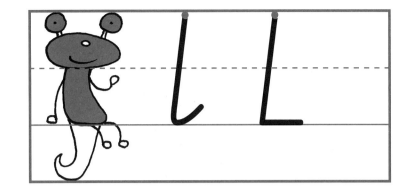

Trace.

Trace.

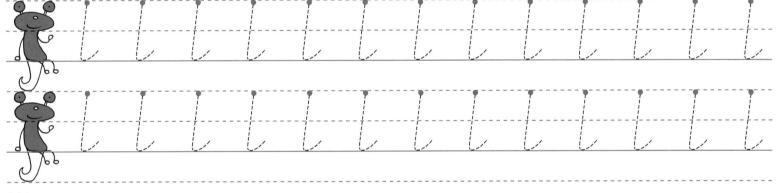

Write.

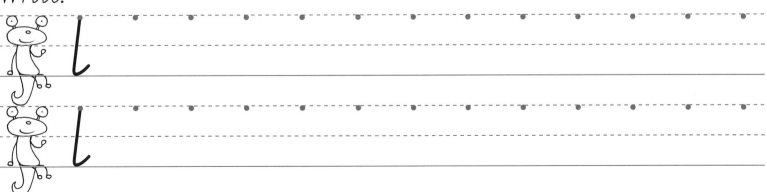

 (Patter) Start at the very top. Draw a line straight down and go up to exit. Keep your pencil on the page.

47

Chant:

jiggly jellyfish
j j j

Trace the pattern.

Trace the pattern. Keep your pencil on the page.

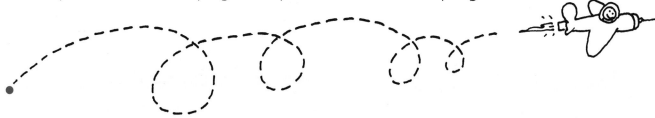

Trace the pattern. Keep your pencil on the page.

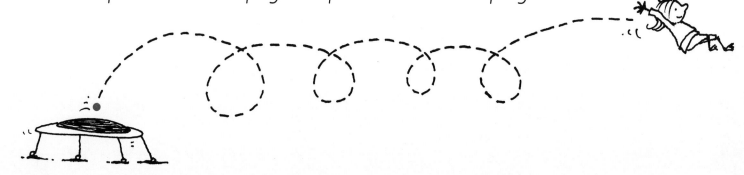

Track.

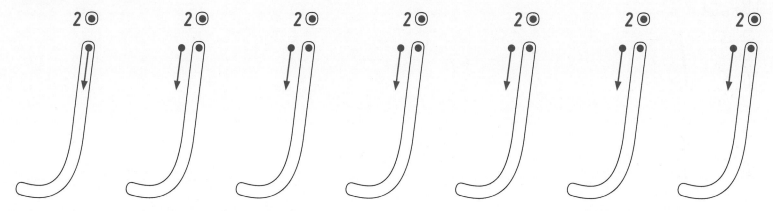

Handwriting: i family letter, body and tail letter (j).
Vocabulary on page: jet, jump, jellyfish, jiggly.
Extra vocabulary: job, just.

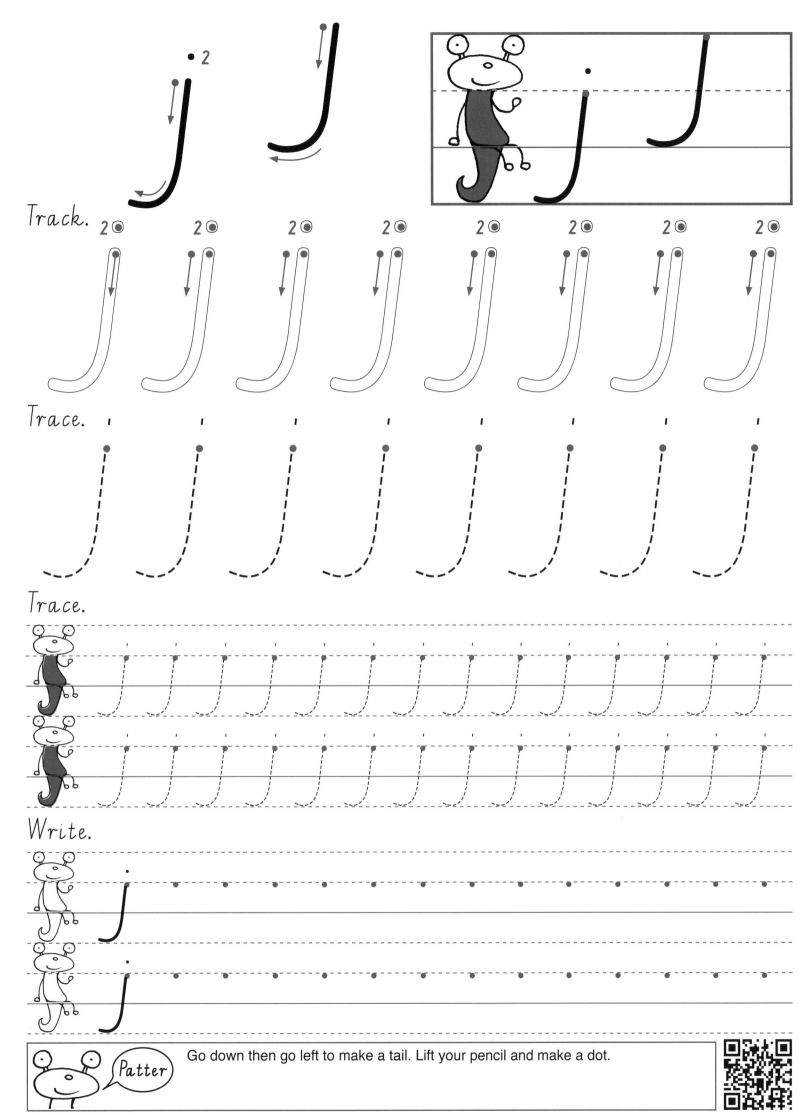

Track.

Trace.

Trace.

Write.

Go down then go left to make a tail. Lift your pencil and make a dot.

ugly undies
u u u

Trace the pattern.

Find u.

u

Trace the pattern. Keep your pencil on the page.

Track.

Handwriting: u family letters, body letter (u).
Vocabulary on page: ugly, undies, umbrella.
Extra vocabulary: up, under, mum, bug, but, shut, duck.

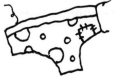  

u U U

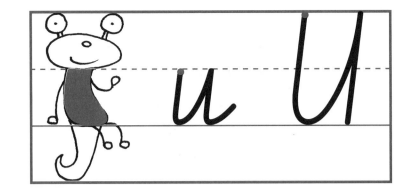

u U

Track.

U U U U U U

Trace.

U U U U U U

Trace.

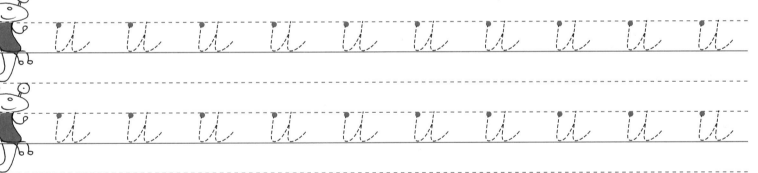

Write.

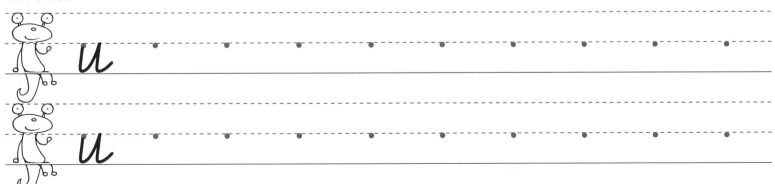

 Patter   Go down, around, up and down, then go up to exit. Keep your pencil on the page.

51

Chant:

yellow yak
y y y

Trace the pattern.

Trace the pattern. Keep your pencil on the page.

Trace the pattern. Turn each pattern into a picture.

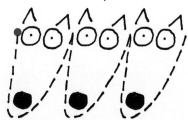

Track.

Handwriting: u family letter, body and tail letter (y).
Vocabulary on page: yak, yellow.
Extra vocabulary: yell, yes, yo-yo.

52

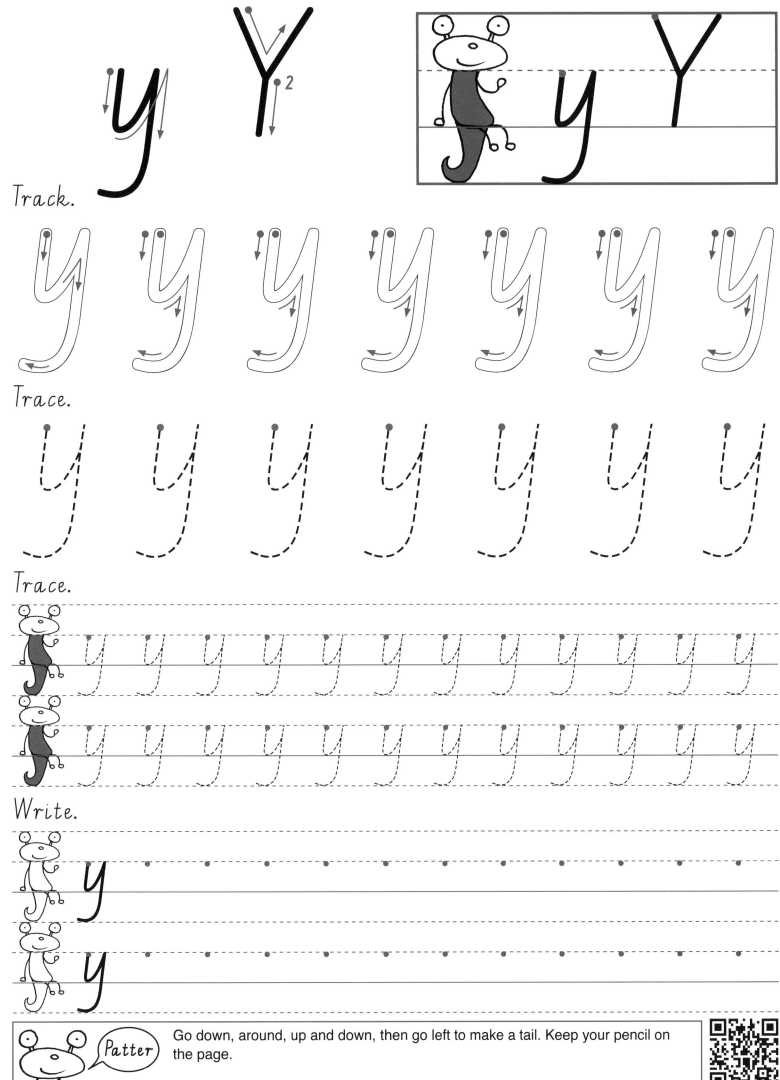

Track.

Trace.

Trace.

Write.

Patter — Go down, around, up and down, then go left to make a tail. Keep your pencil on the page.

Trace the pattern.

Trace the pattern. Keep your pencil on the page.

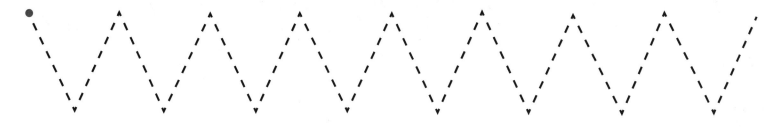

Trace the pattern. Turn each pattern into a picture.

Track.

Handwriting: u family letter, body letter (v).
Vocabulary on page: violin, vulture, vicious.
Extra vocabulary: vet, van, very.

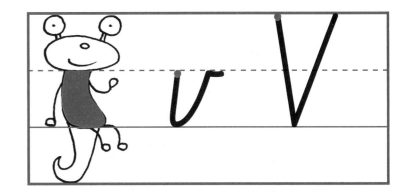

Track.

Trace.

Trace.

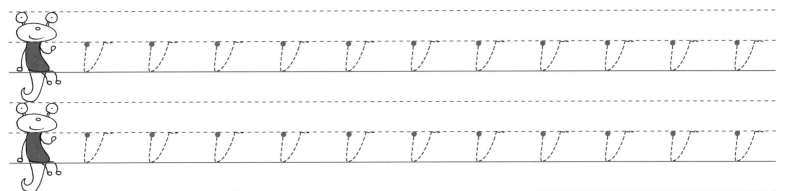

Write.

 Patter — Go down, around and up, then go right to exit. Keep your pencil on the page.

55

Chant:

wiggly wolf
w w w

Trace the pattern.

Trace the pattern. Keep your pencil on the page.

Trace the pattern. Turn each pattern into a picture.

Track.

Handwriting: u family letter, body letter (w).
Vocabulary on page: wiggly, wings, wolf, whale.
Extra vocabulary: wet, win, we, wish, when, where, why.

56

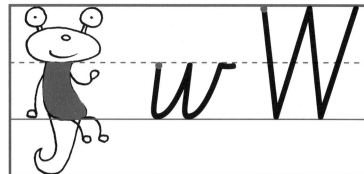

Track.

Trace.

Trace.

Write.

(Patter) Go down, around, up then down again, around and up, then go right to exit. Keep your pencil on the page.

57

BOING

Chant:

bouncy bear

ɬ ɬ ɬ

Trace the pattern.

Trace the pattern.

Trace the patterns.

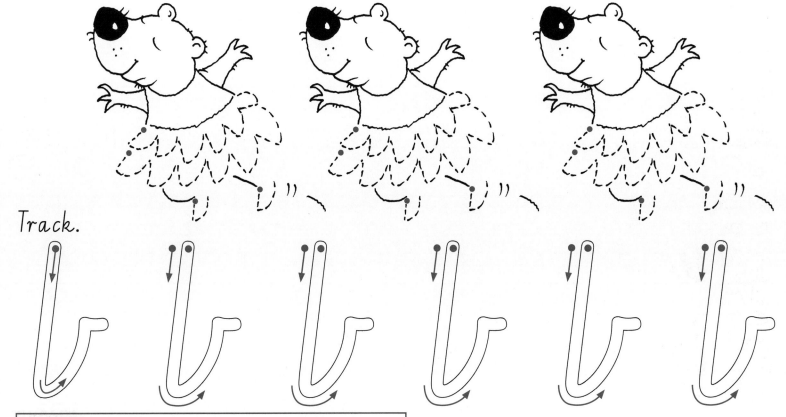

Track.

Handwriting: u family letter, head and body letter (b).
Vocabulary on page: bear, balloon, ballet, bouncy.
Extra vocabulary: be, bee, by, bat, big, bed, but, bug.

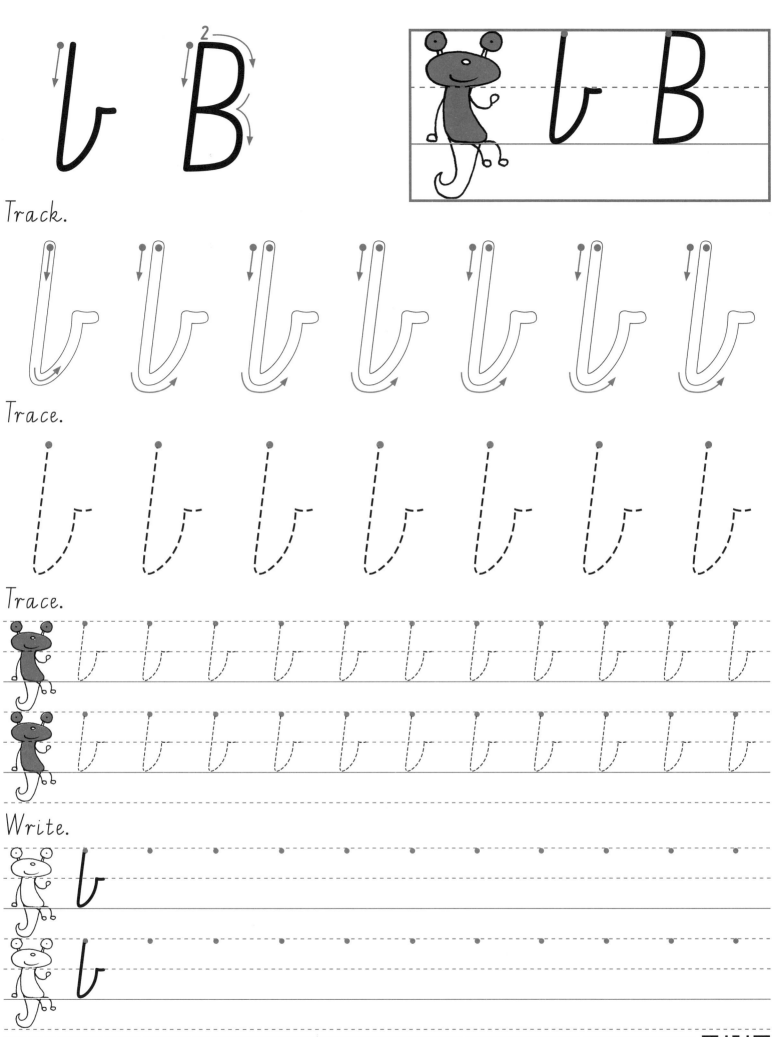

Track.

Trace.

Trace.

Write.

 Patter   Go down, around the bottom and up, then go right to exit. Keep your pencil on the page.

59

one ostrich 1

1

Track.

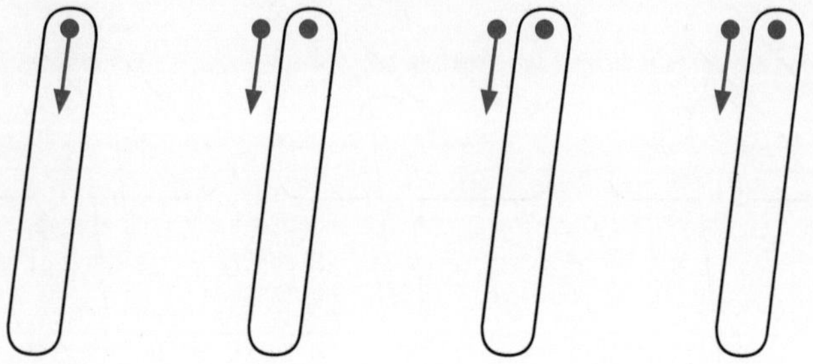

Trace.

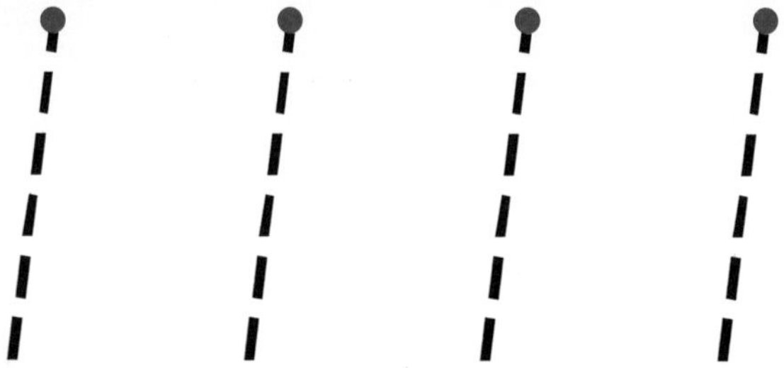

1 1 1 1

Write.

Trace the pattern.

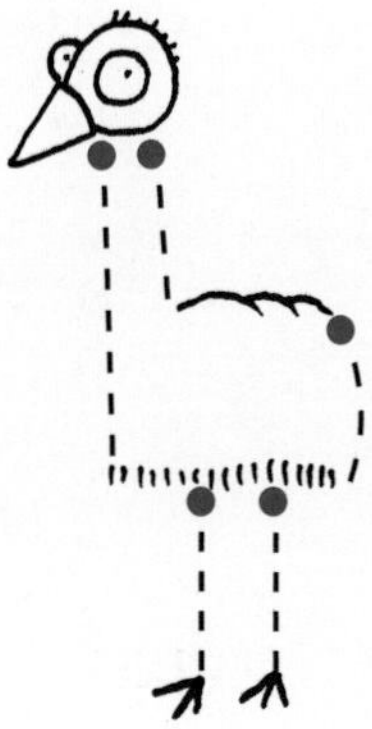

Draw 1 thing.

two tigers 2

2

Track.

Trace.

2 2 2

Write.

Trace the pattern.

Draw 2 things.

three thrushes 3

3

four frogs 4

4

Track.

3 3 3

4 4 4

Trace.

3 3 3

4 4 4

Write.

Write.

Trace the pattern.

Trace the pattern.

Draw 3 things.

Draw 4 things.

five fish 5

5

Track.

5 5 5

Trace.

5 5 5

Write.

• • •

Trace the pattern.

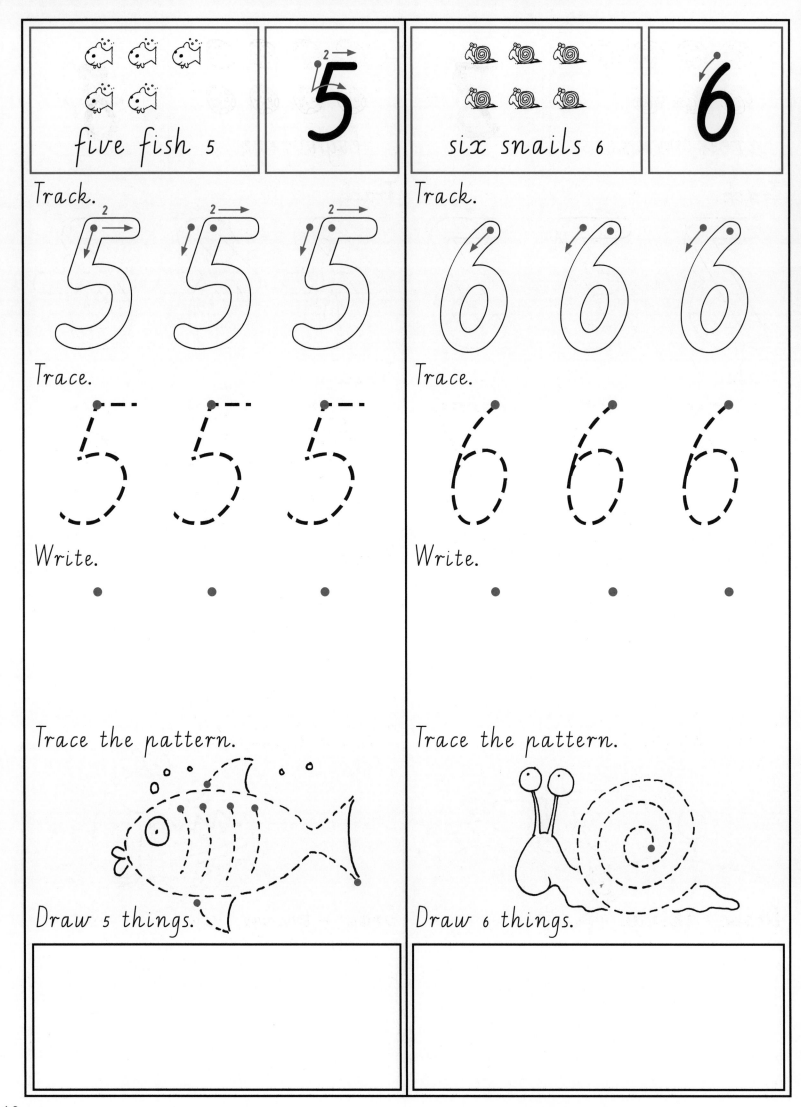

Draw 5 things.

six snails 6

6

Track.

6 6 6

Trace.

6 6 6

Write.

• • •

Trace the pattern.

Draw 6 things.

seven snakes 7

eight eggs 8

Track.

Track.

Trace.

Trace.

Write.

Write.

Trace the pattern.

Trace the pattern.

Draw 7 things.

Draw 8 things.

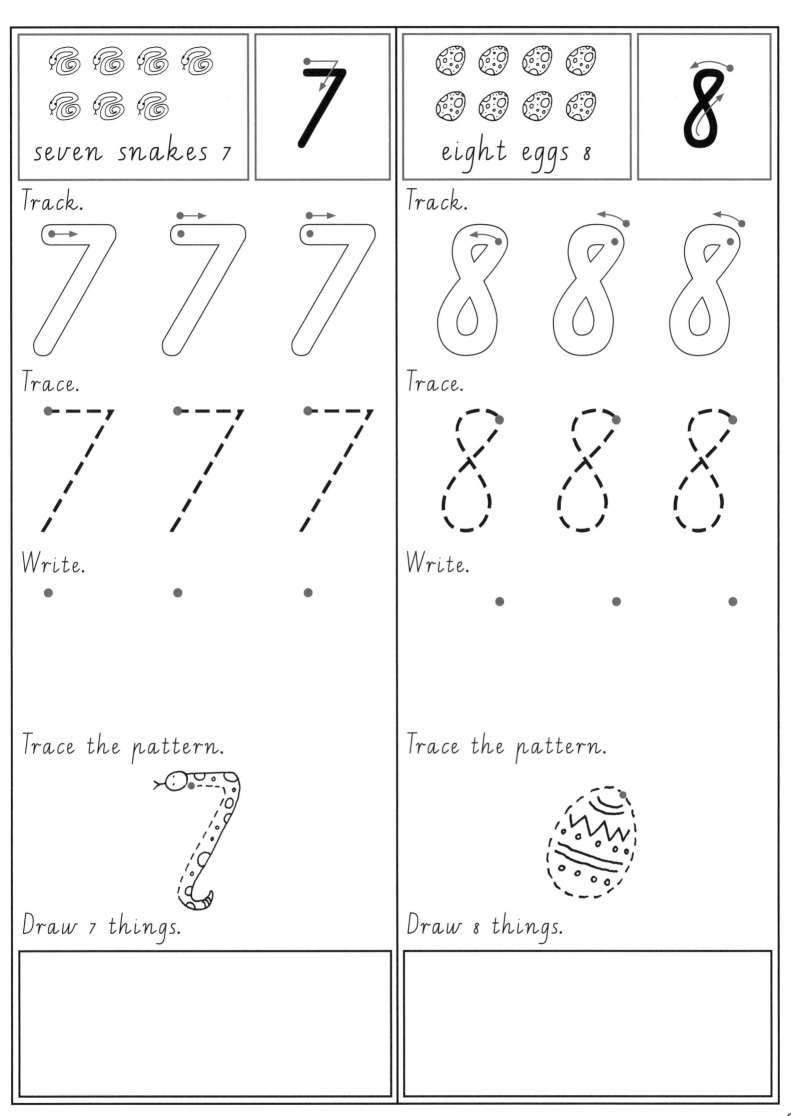

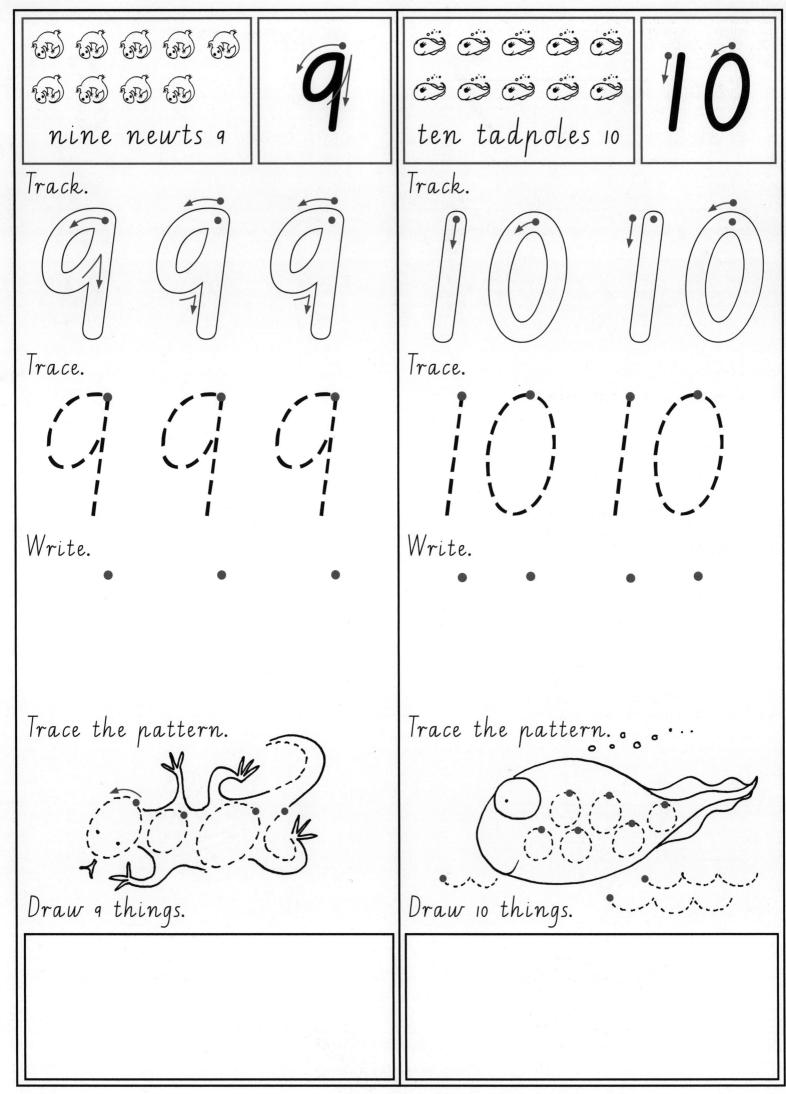

nine newts 9

9

Track.

Trace.

Write.

Trace the pattern.

Draw 9 things.

ten tadpoles 10

10

Track.

Trace.

Write.

Trace the pattern.

Draw 10 things.